For Harry Jonathan Critchfield
with love from J.W.

To Calum
A.R.

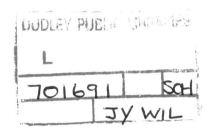

Text copyright © Jeanne Willis, 2006. Illustrations copyright © Adrian Reynolds, 2006.
The rights of Jeanne Willis and Adrian Reynolds to be identified as the author and illustrator of this
work have been asserted by them in accordance with the Copyright, Designs and Patents Act, 1988.
First published in Great Britain in 2006 by Andersen Press Ltd., 20 Vauxhall Bridge Road, London SW1V 2SA.
Published in Australia by Random House Australia Pty., 20 Alfred Street, Milsons Point, Sydney, NSW 2061.
All rights reserved. Colour separated in Switzerland by Photolitho AG, Zürich.
Printed and bound in Singapore.

10   9   8   7   6   5   4   3   2   1

British Library Cataloguing in Publication Data available.

ISBN-10: 1842703358
ISBN-13: 9781842703359

This book has been printed on acid-free paper

WHO'S
IN THE
LOO?

Jeanne Willis
Adrian Reynolds

Andersen Press • London

Who's in the loo?
There's a very long queue.

Is it an elephant having a poo?
They're taking for ever!
Now who could it be?

▼ In Hospital

After nine months in the mother's womb, the new baby is ready to be born. Your mum may go into hospital to have her baby. Your dad may go with her. While the baby is being born, your parents will ask a relative or a close friend to come and look after you.

◀ At Home

Your mum may decide to have her baby at home. A midwife, who is a special person who helps to deliver a baby, may come to help your mum. Your mum and dad may also arrange for a relative or friend to take care of you for a short while.

▶ How Long?

A baby's birth may take only a few hours. Or it can take most of a day. If your mum goes to hospital to have her baby, she may be home a few hours after it is born. Or she may stay in hospital for a few days. It's a big day when the baby comes home at last.

1. Fred's mum was having a baby in hospital. Fred's dad rang to speak to him.

2. The next day Fred went to see his mum in hospital. Fred's mum gave him a special hug.

3. Fred was excited when he saw the baby. His mum let Fred hold him for a while.

How did Fred feel about the birth of his baby brother?

Fred missed his mum when she was in hospital, even though his favourite aunt looked after him. When his dad rang to tell him about his new brother, Fred wasn't sure what he felt. But when he saw his mum, everything felt fine again. Don't worry if your mum goes away to have her baby. She and your dad will soon be home.

▼ Ready to Play?

You may want to play with your new brother or sister straight away. But new-born babies don't play much at first. They mostly sleep and feed. But they do like to be cuddled. Support the baby's head while you are cuddling him or her.

◀ Growing Up

Things change fast with a new baby. After three months the baby will be awake for longer, and will want you to play with him or her. Soon the baby will eat solid food. You might like to help with feeding – it may be messy!

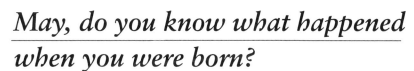

May, do you know what happened when you were born?

"Yes, my mum told me. I was born in hospital. Mum said it took sixteen hours for me to be born. She said she was very pleased when I arrived at last! I've got two younger sisters. They were both born at home. My youngest sister, Jo, only took four hours to be born."

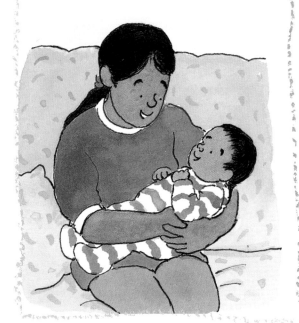

A Newborn Baby

Max's teacher asked everyone in the class to bring in photos of themselves as babies. They stuck the photos on the wall and guessed who was who. No-one guessed which one was Max. Later Max and Rosie talked about babies. Do you know what you were like as a baby? Did you cry or sleep a lot?

A baby feeds from the mum's breast.

Or a baby feeds from a bottle.

▼ Playing With The Baby

Newborn babies are very small at first – but don't be scared to play with them! Babies like to look at people's faces. They learn to talk by copying the sounds we make so sing nursery rhymes and talk to the baby.

Make the baby laugh by being as silly as you like!

◀ Why Do Babies Cry?

Crying is a baby's only way of saying he or she needs something. A baby cries to get attention, if they are hungry or uncomfortable, or bored. Don't feel upset if the baby cries. You may get really good at knowing what the baby wants.

▶ Sleeping Problems

New babies need to feed often, including at night. Your mum and dad will be tired if they get up several times at night.

You may also sleep badly, especially if you can hear the baby crying. There is nothing to worry about, so try to relax at night.

1. Ayisha and her family were very excited. The new baby had just come home.

2. But when friends came round, the baby was the centre of attention. Ayisha felt left out.

3. Later Ayisha talked it over with her mum.

Why was Ayisha upset?

Ayisha was really pleased about the new baby. But she got upset when she felt no-one was taking any notice of her any more. Things may feel different at first with a new baby at home. It will take time to get used to having a little stranger in the family. Talk things over with your mum and dad. Talking about your feelings nearly always helps.

▼ Good Times

You will probably have lots of different feelings about the baby. You may feel really pleased most of the time. You may love to play with the baby, and enjoy bath-times or feeds. You may be best at making the baby laugh.

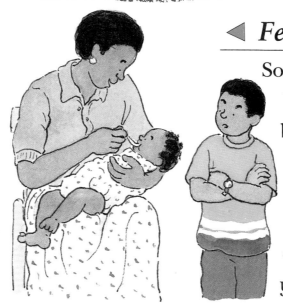

◄ Fed Up?

Sometimes you may feel bored or fed up about the baby. You may feel your mum and dad now have less time for you. Talk to your parents. Perhaps you can agree on a special time for you and your mum or dad.

Max, *what was it like in your family when you were little?*

"My older brother was eight and my sister was four when I was born. Mum said they helped a lot when I was little. They played with me and helped teach me to talk and to read. I learnt to walk quickly so I could keep up with them!"

17

My New Brother Or Sister

May and Dean are showing each other pictures of the people in their families, which they drew at school. Dean said he and his sister, Sonia, play together a lot. May said she used to get on badly with her younger sister, Amy, but now they are good friends. If you've got brothers and sisters, how do you get on with them?

My sister Sonia is really good at making up games.

I get a bit cross when Amy beats me at cards.

Some brothers and sisters get on.

Others seem to fight a lot.

▼ Talking, Walking

Of course, you can do hundreds of things a baby cannot do. Young babies cannot feed themselves or use a potty. But they grow up fast. At six months, a baby may start to crawl. At nine months, he or she may begin to say a few words.

▶ Younger Brothers And Sisters

If you have a younger brother or sister, he or she may not feel as you do about the baby. He or she is more likely to feel angry and a bit left out.

If you spend time with your little brother or sister, it can really help them to feel special, too.

◀ Safety First

Babies have no idea about what is safe. They put things into their mouths to taste them and to see if they are soft or hard. But you know what is not safe to eat, and places that aren't safe to go near. This can really help when you are keeping an eye on the baby.

1. Jack felt that his mum only ever played with his new sister. He felt angry and hit his mum.

2. Jack said his mum didn't care about him. Jack's mum said hitting wasn't allowed.

3. Next time he felt angry, Jack kicked a football. After a while he felt a bit better.

Why did Jack feel angry?

With the new baby, Jack felt cross and left out. Like him, you might feel angry. After all, you didn't choose to have a new baby in your family. You may feel like breaking something or even hitting someone. But this would only make things worse. Talk about your feelings. If you still feel like hitting out, hit something soft, like a cushion, or kick a football outside.

▼ Family Fights

Sometimes you may quarrel with your brother or sister. But you probably stick up for each other when it matters most. Some brothers and sisters quarrel a lot when they are young, but become good friends later.

◀ Sharing

You may feel jealous of your brother or sister. You may find it hard to share your mum and dad.

But just because your parents love your new sister or brother, doesn't mean they will love you any less.

How do you get on with your sisters, May?

"Amy was born when I was three. I felt a bit jealous of her at first. Then, when I was six and Amy was three, Jo was born. I liked playing with Jo, but I could see Amy felt angry. I told Amy I knew how she was feeling. Now Amy and I play together lots."

Don't Forget ...

How do you feel now about the new baby in your family, Rosie?

"At first I didn't like the idea of lots of change. After mum and I talked about it, I felt better. I talked things over with Steve, my stepdad. I'm looking forward to it now. I'm going to help choose the baby's name."

Does a new baby make a big difference to a family, Dean?

"You may feel as if you get your own way less when there is a new baby around. But no-one gets their own way all the time. Having a new baby in our family helped me to see that other people's feelings were important too. It's good, too, because we can have lots of fun now that our family is bigger."

May, do you find it easy to talk things over in your family?

"When my sister Amy was small, for a bit I thought that mum and dad loved her more than me. But I told mum and dad how I felt.

They said that they loved us both just as much, but sometimes Amy needed more looking after because she was a baby."

Do you like having a brother and sister, Max?

"Yeah. It's great. I learned from my big brother and sister. There's a video of my brother teaching me to walk. It's really funny. Now that I'm older, we all have even more fun together."

23

Index

All the photographs in this book have been posed by models. The publishers would like to thank them all.